lifts of the spirit we're all thirsting for."

His aim is not to create a monastic reign of quiet withdrawal: "Obviously, it's important to break our silence and share our cries, share our prayers, with the people in our lives. And when we share our stories we'll grow in understanding of each other because we'll soon discover that we have pretty much the same joys and the same fears. . . . But we must begin by listening to our own cries. The first step is to find a quiet place away from everyone and become silent. The purpose of this book is to help you do this—to begin by hearing my cries and those of the other people found in this book and all over the world."

Cries . . . but Silent will become your "personal property" as few other books have ever done. It is a listening post sensitively, vibrantly tuned to the deepest pulse of love, spirit, joy, sorrow, compassion and the whole range of reverberating "cries" by which God pervades the fabric of our actually very extraordinary lives.

Cries . . .
but Silent

Cries . . .
but Silent

meditations by
Andrew Costello

THE THOMAS MORE PRESS
Chicago, Illinois

ISBN 0-88347-127-2

23331

Table of Contents

TO MY FATHER —
A POET I NEVER REALLY KNEW
TILL AFTER HE DIED —
WHO TAUGHT ME THINGS
I'M ONLY BEGINNING TO REALIZE.

Preface

CRIES – BUT SILENT

Words . . . becoming flesh . . . the cries of a baby becoming the joy of a mother . . . right now . . . somewhere . . . in our world. Be quiet for a moment. Hear the sounds all around you. God is speaking all over the world.

Cries — but silent . . . .

This book is all about God and God's story. It's about God's words, God's cries. This book is all about us and our story — our words and our cries. It's all about those inner conversations constantly going on inside of all of us.

Cries — but silent . . . .

The words, the captured conversations, the meditations that follow might not at times sound religious, but who separated religion from life? There are no secular moments. All moments are grace filled. God wrote the whole story.

Cries — but silent . . . .

11

Where do we get our inspirations from? Where do we find those necessary words, those necessary lifts of the spirit we're all thirsting for? "Out of the depths I cry to you O Lord; Lord hear my voice" (Psalm 130)!

Cries — but silent . . . .

Inspirations, graces, often come at the unexpected moment. We feel like we're drowning because of a family problem and we go to church for the sermon and the pulpit that morning is an empty cup. But suddenly back in our bench after receiving the bread, after drinking the wine, we close our eyes and a shaft of light comes pouring through our stained glass windows within. We experience an in-depth conversation with God. We hear God's voice and we begin to cry and nobody in the church knows the joy within our heart.

Cries — but silent . . . .

Or it's late at night. It's been a long day and we're sitting there at the kitchen table in a robe or a T-shirt. All have gone home or gone to bed. We're alone — deep in a conversation with ourselves — enjoying a cup of tea or decaffeinated coffee and suddenly a remark somebody made that morning hits us. We finally found the piece to a puzzle we didn't know we were working on for years. Or it's the night after a graduation or the last wedding and sitting there sipping on all that happened, we realize that all the sacrifices in raising the children were well worth it. We begin to cry tears of joy. We realize we're not alone. God is with us. People are with us all our days, all over the world.

Cries — but silent . . . .

Obviously it's important to break our silence and share our cries, share our prayers, with the people in our lives. And when we share our stories — we'll grow in understanding of each other — because we'll soon discover that we all have pretty much the same joys and the same fears — the things we're proud of and the things we'd like to throw out in the morning with the garbage.

Cries — but silent . . . .

But we must begin by listening to our own cries. The first step is to find a quiet place away from everyone and become silent. The purpose of this book is to help you to do this — to begin by hearing your own story by hearing my cries and those of the other people found in this book and all over the world.

Cries — but silent . . . .

Andrew Costello, C.SS.R.

SEASONED MAN

Snow running
    and rushing
    in gangs,
    never alone,
    drifting along
    the winter streets
    in cold imitation
    of autumn leaves.

But I in the bold summer
    of my life
    beginning to walk,
    slowly,
    and more deliberately,
    with
        or
            without
    the crowd.

Becoming my own man.

CONFESSION

It was
an empty afternoon
when the Lord
drifted into my life,
into my empty house.

He came and just sat there
on a wooden chair,
and I began sifting
out what I needed:
faith, confidence,
words, healing,
understanding, movement.

He just sat there
and listened to all
I never did.

MY SLOW RESURRECTION

In a world of instant
    breakfast, lunch and pictures,
in the rush hour
    of fast, fast relief
    from minor aches and pains,
some things still take time
    to change,
    to develop,
    to grow:
    me,
    you,
    bread,
    wine,
and the coming of spring.

WHO CARES?

Who cares?
Who really cares?
Who really dares
     to notice me?

Who listens?
Who really listens
     to me?

We all sit
     on our own couches,
     at our own coffee tables,
     inside our own coffee cups.

And I never reached
     for a drop of cream,
     a drop of you.
     I just sit back
     and take my coffee black.

POSSIBILITIES

This planet
is a yellow school bus
climbing the morning hill,
filled with children,
papers and pencils,
possibilities,
and then it passes
the senior citizen bus
going the other way,
possibilities. . . .

SLIDE SHOW

The slides,
click, click,
sliding into
their slots,
fading in,
fading out,
last Christmas,
last wedding,
last summer,
and in
the dark,
come comments,
and laughter,
and sometimes
sudden sorrow,
when someone
who died
suddenly appears,
and all
is silent,
and all
is dark.

SAME STREET

Most of the time
when I picture God,
I picture him
as an old man
up the street,
working on his car,
under the hood,
trying to start his car,
and I'm down here,
running here and there,
and my car rarely
gives me trouble.

AUTUMN EYES

The leaves change
    and color
    and crisp
    and start
    to fade,
Like you,
    but your eyes
    remain young
    and active
    and alive
    this autumn day.
Remember your eyes:
    they tell me
    what your spring
    and summer
    were like.

<pre>
                The
                giant
                economy
size   can   of   earth
sprayed   morning
mist   into
the   whole
winter   world
around   me
and   the
naked   branches
looked   like
antlers   in
the   fog
and   nature
kept   squeezing
and   squeezing
more   and
more   spray
into   the
air   and
named   the
fragrance   Morning   Mist.
</pre>

MICHAEL

Michael,
you left us
all too quickly,
too suddenly.
You left us
all so lonely
in a house
with your memories
and without your presence,
without your jokes,
without your Michaelness.
Your picture on top of the T.V.
will never take your place.
We had no idea
that you would be dead
that Tuesday —
no idea of your cancer.

Did you know?

I can't forget
those few moments
alone with you
in the kitchen,
as we put our dishes

in the sink — the last
time I talked with you.
We don't regret the days,
the 15 years
we had with you, Michael,
but it's the damn missing,
in a house filled with your joy.
I guess that's why
we find ourselves
sitting here crying,
sitting here with the missing,
the missing.

PROBABLE CAUSE

Too early to begin,
too late to dream.
Why am I always
making all these excuses
to cover my nakedness?
Laziness, the original sin,
fills my garden.

STANDING HERE

Concrete legs,
a weight lifter,
holding the bridge up
over the harbor,
straining as you ride
back and forth
from A to B,
rarely noticing me,
my quiet presence,
my cues
now and then,
supporting you,
standing here
under this bridge,
cold concrete,
especially in the night
and in the winter.

o

The sound of "o"
can sound so lonely
when one feels
so alone,
so isolated,
like a widow
with only coffee,
looking down
a cold
November morning.

But sounds
can change,
tombs can open,
and there can be
a knock on the door
every Easter morning.

FRUSTRATION

When frustration
moves in,
it moves
into my
middle floors;

it rents
my stomach,
my heart,
my guts,

and slowly
moves up
and blocks
the stairway
to my mouth,

and so
I have
no way
to tell
you how
I feel,

and this
causes even
more frustration.

PLANETS

Everyone of us
is a sun
with people
like planets
revolving
around us,
depending on us.

And some like Mercury
move so fast
in and out of our lives
because of early deaths
or jobs in distant cities.

And then we have our
Venus and down-to-Earth types,
who are almost
about the same.

But then there
are our Plutos,
those people
in our background
who are always there,
always with us,
from start to finish.

No wonder
the planet Pluto
took so long
to be discovered.

ROOTS

ABOVE
SKY
THE
SEE
AND
THISSIDEWALKOFCEMENT
THROUGH
CRUSH
I'LL
SOMEDAY
SURELY
AND
SLOWLY

MY DAYS ARE NUMBERED

Me,
    with thousands
    and thousands
    of days
    come out
    of my cocoon
    and return
    after dark
    with trivia
    under my arm,
    loudly announcing,
    "I've found it!"
    and all my friends
      wondering
    behind my back,
    "What will he
      be reaching for
      next week,
      next month,
      next year?"

Then the moth appears
with three days of life
and behind my back
quietly searches
and reaches after Light.

ADAM

Dried up leaves
rushing down autumn streets,
snow swirling
across macadam highways,
encased in a frozen waste,
a non-skier
conning myself for a moment
to watch the moon
cast a fluorescent glow
on the snow;
but most of the time
naked,
under a barren fig tree
without leaves.
I long for resurrection
and the road towards spring,
towards a new garden
of delights.

37

thirty — seven
people in
a circle,
eating words
and joy
and pain;
passing each
other around
like a
bowl of
pretzels and
out of
somewhere comes
the laughing
burp "There's
enough people
here for
everybody."

STARING

Staring —
You catch me
Staring,
Right in your face.

And not even
Not pretending
To listen
To you.

Just staring —
And not even
Not into space.

And you —
You're wondering,
Aren't you?

You're thinking
It's you.

No. — You're boring,
But you just
Can't get into
My space.

RE-RUN

Night after night
he sat there
all alone
watching the cold air
hanging around the street light.
Bored by the black and white
late show.
It was an old movie anyhow.
The silent phone,
the door,
the morning,
nothing interested him,
except the cold air
surrounding the mercury light
shining on the street below.

THE LAST CAR

The light turned red,
    so I stood there
    on the corner,
    waiting for the traffic
    to go by.

The light turned green,
    so I stood there,
    because just then
    my eye noticed
    a funeral procession
    going by.

First the hearse,
    then two black Cadillacs
    then the long line
    of slow cars,
    lights on,
    with everyone
    seated silently
    behind closed windows,
    women with purses
    on their laps,
    with handkerchiefs
    cupped to their eyes.

The light turned red
    and the cars
    moved slowly
    down the street
    where the dead person
    must have lived.

The light turned green,
    but instead of moving
    I just stood there
    as I read
    the license plate
    on the last car,
    CRY — 456.

DIARY

Before you come down
from the mountain,
write it down fast, clearly, quickly,
before it fades, before it's too late.

Line up the words.
Carve them in stone.
Number them in your journal.
Show them in your face, in your eyes.

Make them last,
these results of your inner mumblings,
these commandments you've heard
during long bus rides,
these commandments you've discovered
from lonely mistakes, or
from being misquoted, or
from being misunderstood.

Tell everyone that after
all these years of not knowing,
you finally know
that your real goals so far were:

1)   to be loved,
2)   to be accepted,
3)   to know you know you have something to offer,
4)   to know they know you have something to offer,

5) to know they know you know,
6) to know you're still learning,
7) to know that each fall teaches if you rise,
8) to know you're beginning to realize there are others,
9) to know you're beginning to know there is a God,
10) to know there's more to know.

But remember,
these ten will be broken,
will be forgotten,
will some day seem adolescent,
but at least you've written them down,
you've chiseled them in stone.

Remember,
new commandments,
new insights,
will begin to appear,
after they have rumbled around in your mind
for a while as you move across the desert.

Remember,
in your next exodus,
on your next mountain,
you might begin to carve,
slowly and quietly
the word "love",
but this time on a tree.

WORDS

Kindness and truth
justice and love,
are nice words,
but how much nicer are:
Billy and Mary,
Jerry and Peggy,
and you too, Joanne.

CANCER

The night was bright
because of the glistening
Passover moon.
I lay there awake
listening to both my
pulse and my watch,
wondering which would
stop first,
knowing that soon
my hour would come,
knowing that my Judas body
had betrayed me,
with cancer kissing
and killing all my insides.
For weeks
I cried with anger
at this creeping way
to die, this agony
in a bed called Gethsemane,
unable to flee the fears
pulsing down the valley
of my ear, this crucifying night,
not even wanting to roll over
and reach for the cup
of water on the table,
unable to escape death,
yet slowly I hear
myself beginning to
utter my first
word, "Father. . . ."

THE SYSTEM

Waiting,
Waiting on a long subway platform,
Waiting
for a train.
Feeling
all alone.
Looking down the long tracks,
        down the long dark tunnel.

Hoping
for some sound,
    some signal,
    some light
down the long dark tunnel,
telling me
a train is coming,
coming to take me home.

Suddenly,
while standing there,
I notice that everybody
on both sides of the track
is doing the same thing,
looking down the long tracks,
looking.

But why
are we all so quiet,
        all so silent?

BIRTHDAY

The present
is always
you.

EMPTY MARRIAGE

She began to think that
everything seemed so empty
this morning
as she threw
the wrinkled tube
of tooth paste
at the waste basket
next to the sink
and the toilet flushed
as she walked out
past the empty bed
where he snored
and she wondered
as she dressed
what time
he came in last night
and where he was
as she headed
for the kitchen
with an empty scotch bottle
and a glass
all the time
wondering.

IT'S IN ME

It's in me.
I know it.
I always knew it.
It's in me.

Where and when
and what it is
I don't know,
but it's in me.

"It's in me."
Those three words
keep haunting me,
keep echoing in me.

It's in me,
but I keep saying
it's the phone,
and these unexpected door bells,
or these knockings on the door
that stop me,
that block me
from discovering
what's in me.

It's in me,
along with the excuses
and the pride and the fears
to ask for help,
but one of these days
I'm going to discover
just what it is
that's in me.

GOD UPON THE WATER

God
do I
ever
really
think of you,
except
perhaps
on rainy days,
when thoughts of you
come running down
the windshield
of my mind?

God,
there I am
driving along
the street
and suddenly
you blur my vision
with storm
or gentle rain,
and even then
I turn to wipe
you off my mind.

UNINVITED GUEST

Fear steps into
     the bedroom
     of my heart
     without knocking,
     and just sits there
     on the edge
     of my bed,
     waiting,
     without even taking
     its dark coat off.

While out front in
     my living room,
     my mask
     shakes hands,
     takes coats,
     makes jokes,
     serves drinks,
     then dinner,
     and finally
     closes the door.

Then I stand there
     holding the door knob,
     wishing I could leave
     with the guests,
     knowing I have to go back
     and see
     what's on its mind,
     and whether or not
     I'll ask it to stay
     the dark night.

WEDDING LIST

Invitations,
Transactions,
Double dealings,
Your aunt
for my uncle.
Uh, oh!
These three
can't be
at the same table.
Divorces
are inevitable.

SUPERMARKET

Entrance and Exit.
Life would be so easy
if that's all it was.
The stepping on those
automatic floors,
the passing through
those automatic doors.
Birth to Death.
But it's the in between
isn't it?
The aisles,
the shelves,
the choices,
and all you have is one cart,
a husband waiting outside
in the car,
children,
sometimes a small child,
and $84.23

CHRIST

He is bread cast
upon the waters,
calling to us
inside our frightened boat,
inside our frightened skins,
"It is I; do not be afraid."

HIT AND RUN

Came up over a hill
and my stomach
and my eyes
veered to the right
at the sight of a dog
somebody else
from the other direction
had just hit and crippled.
And the red flowed
over the icy road,
and although my window
was sealed tight,
protecting me
from the January cold,
I projected screams
from its mouth.
And I couldn't stop.
I left it there,
feeling guilty
all the way home —
The Bad Samaritan —
hit and run,
some kid's dog,
still lying there
in my real view mirror.

OBVIOUSLY

The meeting
never takes
place at
the meeting.
It takes
place at
the coffee
break and
over drinks
and over
the phone,
afterwards, but
only afterwards.

FAST FOOD CHAIN

Looking back now
alone at this table
in the corner,
feeling stupid,
playing with the salt
and pepper shakers,
bringing them closer and
closer to each other,
realizing now how blind
I was that day I left
the ring—the circle of our love—
beginning to eat fast,
on the run—standing up—
refusing to sit and talk
when you ran to me,
letting the fantasy of freedom
blur my ability to
see what you mean
to me, letting laziness
be canned and labeled
as "gotta be me",
joining the crowd of singles
standing at bars, eating
at fast food chains,
instant everything, a network
of lonely people, joining
a chain gang, imprisoned
by my refusal to admit
I'm not alone, forgetting
that maybe if we sat down
and had a meal together,
slowly . . . maybe . . . something
might matter . . . between us.

SUBWAY

Deep
below the surface
below the streets,
below the city's skin,
cans of people
ride along quietly,
glide alone silently,
the factory conveyor belt,
towards home,
towards supper.

Deep people,
holding onto handles,
holding onto papers,
holding onto dreams,
handed to them
in those subway advertisements,
paging through everything
that happened to them since
they left for work
this morning.

Deep
below the surface,
below the skin,
cans of people
without labels,
without emotions,
but inside
filled with stories and commotions
waiting to get home
to be opened for supper.

CELIBACY

To be a celibate
is to be one's own son.
To be a young man
is to be a dreamer.
To be a father
is to have a son.
He'll be the one,
the one to carry on
one's unreachable dreams.
But to be a celibate
is to be one's own son,
the one to carry on
one's unreachable dreams.

BATHROOM SCALE

Some minds
have a
bathroom scale
to sneak to,
to step on,
to weigh
the words,
the comments
of the day,
still nibbling
on a comment,
(or was it
an innuendo?),
starving for
the box
of chocolates,
always hungry
for any kind
of approval,
or rejection,
constantly
weighing,
weighing,
weighing.

OLD PERSON'S ROOM

It was a museum
     of chairs
     and afghans,
and photos, photos,
     everywhere,
a store with shelves
     of memories,
     pictures,
     and souvenirs
     of Rome
     and California,
     and what looked
     like a Pieta
     from the New York
     World's Fair.

And after ten minutes
     of sipping
     coffee and stories
     all I began
     to notice
     were her eyes —
     her eyes
     that kept on talking,
     that kept on smiling.

WORN

Women twisting rings,
turning them round
and round just as
planes were about
to leave the ground,
or during sermons,
or waiting for lovers
at bars,
in cars,
waiting for trains
with husbands,
with supper
on the stove
back home,
slowly burning,
slowly wearing out.

8:49 P.M.

Sometimes
all we
can say
to each
other is
"Thank you."

WILLOWS

The weeping
willows
brushed against
the tombstones
and together with
time and the rain
erased the names
of the dead.

TO BREATHE

S   P   A   C   E
SPACE
SP   AC   E
SPA   CE
S   PACE
SPACESPACESPACESPACESPACE

MISS SUITCASE

Kept in the closet,
Stuck in the basement
      of planes,
While you fly first class.

Forgotten,
Used,
Forgotten again,
Abused,
Shoved under beds,
Banged around.

Well, someday soon
You're going to
      stand there
      stupid,
At your airport merry-go-round,
      waiting for me.

And me,
Sir Prize,
I'll be on another flight.

AIRPORT

Strangers in this enormous
        waiting room,
Strangers in this world
      of arrivals
      and departures,
Expectant fathers and mothers,
      walking back
        and forth,
      constantly checking
        time and tickets,
Expectant children,
      just sitting here
      in this red-rugged
      womb,
      quietly watching
      and waiting
      to be born
      to newer worlds.

MY GOD

My God just sits there
    like my father
    in his corner chair
    reading his paper,
    silently listening
    and watching everything
    that is going on.

My God just sits there
    like my father
    in the back seat
    of my car,
    silently watching
    the speedometer
    and how I drive the car.

But my father died
    before I went over
    to sit with him
    in his corner chair,
    before I invited him
    into the front seat
    of my car.

76 YEAR OLD NUN

Once upon a time
a small girl walked
into a church
and walked up to the front
and looked up at God
and asked,
"God, what's it like to be God?"

And a voice said,
"Do you have time?"

And the little girl said, "Yes!"

And for the next 70 years
the girl sat there in church
listening to God's answer.

KNOWLEDGE EXPLOSION

I rarely notice
those tiny airplanes
crawling across
the top pane
of my window,
or that the heel
of my left shoe
is wearing thin,
or that my
cholesterol level
has been a bit too high
since November,
or that the real reason
for all this study
to get my Ph.D.
is to make up
for my father's failures,
and to beat my brother,
who only got a Master's Degree.
Ugh. I wish I could fly away.

DID YOU EVER

Did you ever
come up a hill
in mid-January
and the sides
of the road
are old snow
and ugly dark ice,
but suddenly
the clouds split
and the afternoon sun
casts a red glow
on a certain type
of tree, whose
branches look like red
roots upside down
hanging in mid-air?

Did you ever
come to a point
of despair in
mid-life, where
you feel uprooted,
and the road
backwards and forwards
looks like ugly dark ice,
but suddenly you find yourself
sitting in an afternoon church,
and the sun breaks
through the grey and the
dark stained glass windows,
and the crucified hanging
in mid-air above the altar,
casts that certain red glow?

QUIET

Angry
because
You are
so silent,
so quiet,
like an electric clock,
spanning time
forever Future,
and sometimes
when I'm quiet
I realize
that when
it comes to You
it's me
who is
so silent,
so quiet.

THE GROUP

Turning the pages,
looking at photos
taken so long ago,
I came upon a picture,
a captured day from yesterday.

We were at the beach.
In the background
you can see miles of water
rolling in.
We were young then,
no wrinkles,
no double chins,
posing in the bathing suits
of our youth, the masculine
and feminine,
all of us holding onto
each other for a moment,
then the "smile",
and then we broke
for games,
for marriages,
for journeys
across the waters,
never to be pictured together again.

TOGETHER

Walking,
watching
a lone dark bird
standing high
in an empty tree,
late winter,
not yet spring,
and he was
watching me
walking down
the cold macadam road,
both of us
wondering
why we were so far
away from the others.

NON-ADDICTION

Sitting there,
            staring there,
the non-addict
            just sits there,
staring at staring
            with an empty eye.

Addicted to nothing,
            no wine,
            no women,
            no song.

Needing something,
            anything,
needing an overdose
            of life and love,
needing an overdose
            of someone,
to come over to fix,
            to fill the nothing,
            to fill the staring,
            to fill the empty eye.

STARS

Millions and millions
        of stars
        in the night,
        all lights,
all glittering,
        like people
        at a party,
all looking so close,
        but like the stars
        so far apart,
        burnt out,
        or reflecting
        the light
        of others.
And we the party goers,
        gazing at the stars,
        watching and wondering
        who is
        orbiting
        around whom,
touching in the night.

RIPPLE

Calm,
water,
a leaf
lying on a pond,
my soul
till You
moved into
my stillness.

CUT

That remark you made
       last month
       scratched my mind.

And I keep picking
       the scab off.

Never telling you
       to heal the cut,

Never telling you
       that it hurt,

Never telling you
       I can't forgive you

Yet. . . .

PIETA

Sitting in the back
of the church I began
watching a young mother
holding her handicapped
daughter in her arms
and just then the priest
in the distance said,
"This is my body . . . .
    This is my blood . . . ."

CHANNEL

Evidently
my ratings
have slipped.

You flip
past me,
never checking
me out.

Am I a re-run?

Or do you think
I'm off the air?

Have you checked
to see if I'm
worth watching?

What are you after,
Looker?

SIGNS

It wasn't till I learned to drive
        that I began to see
        all those signs
        along the way,
        STOP,
        SLOW DOWN,
        YIELD,
        DO NOT ENTER.

It wasn't till I was thirty-five
        that I began to hear
        all those warnings,
        BE CAREFUL,
        BE PRUDENT,
        THIS IS THE WAY WE DO IT
        AROUND HERE,
        IF YOU DON'T LIKE IT,
        LEAVE.

But it wasn't till I began to pray
        that I was able
        to leave that DEAD END,
        and now I know
        that with God
        I'm the one
        who sets the speed,
        who writes the signs,
        who marks the roads,
        and directs the traffic
        of my life.

YOU NEVER ASKED

Both of them
felt like they were in their seventies.

She was 58.
He was 62.

They had been married
"too many years".

He felt like he was losing control.
She felt like he was slipping away.

He noticed that the younger men
were taking away his titles
at work and in the community.

He felt like a failure
because one of his kids
was on drugs drifting away
on a sea of nothingness.

She felt alone because
all the kids had moved away
and two of them had stopped
going to church.

And the house was big and silent.

She had forgotten
long ago "how to be a wife".
All she knew was
that she was mom.

The thought of death
began to surface in both of them,
especially with the increasing number
of funerals they had to attend.

But neither told the other.

"Why scare her?"

"Why give him something else to worry about?"

They did not want to hurt each other.

"I didn't know you were thinking like that."

"You never asked."

"Well, you never asked me, either!"

EVENTUALLY

Santa Claus must take
        off his suit,
        the clown
        his mask.

And eventually the late show
        ends and then
        we all must face
        the All Alone.

SHAPES

Shapes —
      still life —
surround me,
      the roll of thread
      left on the coffee table,
      the clock on my desk,
      the book over there,
and then suddenly
      you walk
      into the room
and I know there is
      still life.

CUP OF LIFE

Holding you
my cup of coffee,
warming myself
with memories of you.
Sipping you
each morning,
sitting here
all alone,
so far away,
remembering
so many days,
aftertastes of you.

HOLY THURSDAY

A table and some chairs,
some bread and some wine,
some words of love and
some words of mystery.

And you take the bread
and you take the wine,
and then you feed us
with your life — and
isn't that enough?

Isn't that enough?

And as I sit there
slowly chewing and sipping
on that haunting question,
I hear the answer, "No."

And I know that I too
must give up my body
and give up my blood,
and have you pick me up and say,
"This is my body and
this is my blood
which will be given up
for all. Do this in
remembrance of me."

GOOD FRIDAY AFTERNOON

It's Good Friday afternoon
and each year
the people pour into church
and stare up at the cross,
and then like blood
drip out of church,
flowing out the doors,
down the steps,
into the streets,
into the world.

HOLY SATURDAY

It was such a silent day,
an empty day without Him.
We all sat so next to each other,
and yet so far away.
The room was like
a funeral parlor
ten minutes before it closes
for the night.
As we kept watching the closed door
we bit our nails wondering what
was happening on the other side
of the world.
With each sound
came more fears
and more frustrations.
Yet there was always
that doubt and so
we waited for the dawn.

EASTER MORNING

Christ
reached me
at the right point,
the right spot,
a crossroads,
when I needed
something or
someone new,
someone beyond
my skin.

Later on
I found out
that he too
was seeking
something,
someone new.

It was me.

His word,
his seed,
his roots,
his power
burst through the concrete floor of my cellar,
breaking through the foundations of my life.

It was a resurrection morning
and all my excuses lay naked,
a skin shed on the floor.

His light,
his radiance,
his transparency
sparkled in my tomb,
exposing my nerves,
my sins,
and all the deepest hopes I ever had for life.

I felt new,
a crying baby,
born once again.

I met Jesus
for the second time,
the poet,
genesis and revelation,
enigma and omega,
friend and stranger,
food and drink,
and we both stood up
and headed for the cellar door —
ready to walk out
to a newer world.

NEXT

The second hand
moves forward.
Doors open,
doors close.
The nurse,
the butcher,
the barber,
the hair dresser,
the disc jockey,
and then God,
yells, "Next!"

FINALLY

This faded photograph
once so new,
once so anxiously
waited for,
like your birth,
finally arrived home
in its Kodak envelope.

Your picture was passed
around the room
and then so soon
found its way
into a dark room,
the forgotten corner
of a bottom drawer,
till your re-birth today

You're finally developed.

WATCH

From time to time
I've wondered
if our marriage
was going to make it.
There were the times
I've waited, waited,
hearing only the heartbeat
of my watch, wanting
to give up on you,
because of forgotten phone calls,
moments of neglect,
the silent arguments,
the lonely questions
in the night.
But then I'd watch you
for three or four days
to see if you
simply forgot to wind
our stopped time together
and now you were ready
to make our old marriage new,
to put our first marriage first.

BUT

I sit here
in the pack
waiting my turn.
Sitting here
watching people
puffing away
at life,
half-lived cigarettes
everywhere,
outside churches,
outside bars,
outside doors,
crushed on floors,
half-smoked lives.
But how much longer
till I leave the pack,
till I catch fire?
But how much longer?

CEMETERY CANOPY

The rain forced us
all into one spot,
united under this canopy.

Death can do that.

The downpour wouldn't
stop, so too the tears
and the silence.

Her death did that.

SIMPLICITY PATTERN

Time,
and the scissors,
and the razor blade of pain
kept cutting away
the non-essentials,
the unnecessary,
till suddenly
I figured out
the pattern —
more and more of you, God
in the fabric of my life.

SIGNALS

The smoke stack
        in the distance
        sends out a silent
        signal
        that all is working.

The toaster
        on the kitchen table
        sends out an early warning
        signal
        that it's about to pop.

And you,
        what signal should I
        be looking for?

STAINED GLASS

You only seem to notice
my outside — my lines —
the dark side of my life.

Why not take another look?
Come inside my chapel
and see me in a new light.

FROZEN MEAT

She kept
her feelings
in the freezer,
a solid lump,
wrapped in aluminum foil.

And yet
she wonders
if she opens up
and lets them thaw out,
will she be burnt?

PSYCHOLOGIST

She kept on saying,
"I'm trapped!
 I feel trapped!
 I don't see any doors.
 I don't see any way
 out of here. I'm trapped.
 I'm trapped."

Then I said,
"Well, you got in . . . ."

But then
should I say,
"You can get out"?

Or do I say,
"Well, together let's look
for a door"?

But if I do that,
then will I be trapped?

DINNER FOR TWO

You sit there
                    two feet away,
as I sit here
twisting
my spaghetti,
wondering,
"Who are you?"

Hidden behind
those glasses,
peeking out
from behind
that curtain
of hair,
water bug eyes
dashing across
the surface
of the room.

Are you scared?

Do you know
what you look like?

You look like
the bird
I saw this morning
on my frozen back lawn,
eating my bread,
but constantly
checking the rest
of the restaurant,
ready to fly.

FORGE AHEAD

The old men
    sit there
    and tell
    me that
    the only way
    to go
    is through
    the mill,
implying that
    all else
    is fake,
    is forgery.

And I,
    standing here,
    smile, then
    walk away
    forging
    the future
    as I go
    with stubborn will,
denying that
    all else
    is fake,
    is forgery.

FEAR

Jogging . . .
a dirt road . . .
a dog named Fear
came running after me
and I froze,
till suddenly
his rope braked him.
Yet
those black skid marks
still remain on my brain
and now
I keep running . . .
running past
all those homes,
all those dogs,
always hoping
that everyone
wears a long rope
round their neck —
tied to a tree.

PARK BENCH

The bench
sat there
all winter
waiting for
children,
waiting for
lovers,
but had to settle
for two old men
in late spring.

PINE BED

In the deep woods
       I came upon
       a pine bed,
       a sanctuary
       of quiet,
       a place of peace
       in the autumn
       of my life.

And as I stood there
       I began to know
       You are always
       here — The Quiet One.

FEELINGS

Not like a load of wash
     that you can stop
     and hang out
     in the wind
     or put in
     the automatic dryer.

Not like anything
     you've said so far,
     but keep on trying
     to understand
     what it feels like
     to have this heavy
     load of wash
     rumbling and swirling
     inside of me.

SELF-DECEPTION

Beneath
the front door
of my car
the corrosion
sets in —
slowly eating away
the body.

Yet I
blindly look
the other way
each day,
rejecting the cancer
underneath my feet,
blind to the rust,
deaf to the deception
that I am rejecting,
growing old.

COMMUNION

Me,
the result
of Communion
of mom and dad
and love and God,
and then
me,
and then
Communion
with family
and friends,
and then
the world
of food
and toys
and Christmas,
and playgrounds,
and school
and Bread and Wine,
and then Communion
with some special people
who brought me
Communion
with God.

NOT KNOWING

Nervous,
not knowing if I hurt you.

Confused,
not knowing if you're angry.

Unsure,
not knowing if I should call you.

Wondering,
not knowing if you're writing
these same words.

THE SECOND DAY

The first day of school
    is never the problem,
    the day our eyes
    like marbles rolled
    around the room,
    a new game.

But it's the second
    and the third
    and the fourth day
    of school,
    of work,
    of marriage,
    of retirement. . . .

When our eyes
    start to drift,
    to lose
    the wonder,
    the newness
    of it all.

MEET THE PRESS

Imagine if each of us
had to
Meet the Press,
Face the Nation,
concerning the
Issues and Answers
of our life.

How would I do?

If I sat there
that night
and watched a re-run
of my answers,
how would I feel?

What's my program,
my vision,
my day to day plan
for our world?

What am I doing
to improve
the environment,
the noise level,
the atmosphere
around me?

What am I doing
about energy,
the handicapped,
the poor,
food shortages,
waste?

How good a job am I doing with my talents?

Am I living up to my promises,
especially the ones I make to myself?

What would be my ratings
in the polls:
75% think I'm doing a good job,
or would it be that only 25%
think I'm doing a good job?
Is it higher or lower?

Would I be re-elected
for another 2, 4, 6 years
of life?

YOU AND ME

You can't have everyone and everything.
You're limited. You're like me.

You have to share your parents, your food,
your space and time with me.

You have to think of me when you turn
your radio on. Maybe I'm trying to get
some extra sleep. What about when you
take a shower? There's only so much
hot water? What about towels?

You can't drive at any speed or any way
you want. I might be on the road.

What about last week when you were at
the restaurant? You just sat there.
I was waiting for you and your chair.
I too had a schedule to keep.

Do you ever see me, hear me,
know that I too am here?

Do you realize that I too have a center,
a culture, thoughts and feelings
and especially a first name?

Do you know that I also have thoughts
about life—about things that I have
been thinking about for years?

Did you ever think to ask me?

Do you know that I worry about being
wrapped up too tightly in myself,
that I fear being too self-centered?

Do you know that I find it difficult
at times to recognize you, because
you never seem to get beyond
your plate and your stories?

Do you realize that it hurts when you yawn
in my face or when you turn back to your
newspaper when I begin to speak?

I'm trying to
listen to you?

Are you trying
to listen to me?

THE BIRD

Always ready
like a bird on a nervous branch
to dart off
to your regular
hiding place
in the bushes,
beyond people,
always ready
to avoid
looking me
in the eye,
never talking
about the stuff
deep in the dark bushes.

HANG UP

Slowly
the music
and the harmony
and the honey
stopped flowing.

And she began
to nag and sag,
cancering away
at him,
at them.

And she's always
on the phone
with someone else,
just when he wants
someone else.

And she just
won't hang up.

And both
continue
making busy signals
and wrong numbers,
heading for the day
they decide
either to hang up
or call each other.

IN THE DARK

Suddenly
candles
are making a come-back.

Suddenly
people
are turning
off their lights
and turning onto candles
in the dark,
casting light and fire
into lovers' eyes,
with desires flowing
through wine glasses,
and the young
are lighting candles
with their drugs and their music,
and the churches are almost empty,
except for mothers
lighting candles
in the dark afternoon aisles
for their children,
lovers and addicts.

WRECKS

Just drove by
a dozen
wrecked cars
just sitting there
in a body shop lot.

Sorry, I couldn't help
but stereotype them
as a dozen
lonely and late night
people at a singles' bar.

SALAD DRESSING

Married
to you
for seven long years
I began
to notice
that you had begun to pick.

It took me 2 hours
to prepare supper,
yet you said I forgot
your favorite salad dressing,
and for the rest of the meal,
and the rest of the year,
I began to pick up signals
that love had moved
out of the house
and began staying
away from home
later and later
into the night.

SISYPHUS

The blue hills
should be green
and the light
shouldn't be pink,
but they are,
standing here
this evening,
this moment
before the night
on this slope
overlooking
the end
of a life.

LOVE HANGS THERE

I spoke the words
in big bright letters.

In fact I underlined them
with slowness.

"Be of love a little
more careful than anything."

But nobody seemed to be impressed
by these words of E. E. Cummings.

Didn't they ever experience God
and then walk away?

Didn't they ever hurt a friend
because of negligence or betrayal?

Didn't they ever love?

Well, now I understand
the reason for banners and posters.

I guess we need to let some words
hang around for a long, long time
on the walls of our minds,
sort of like a crucifix.

Then maybe
we'll start to understand them.

Be of words a little
more careful than anything?

No, but be careful of them;
some become flesh.

CERAMIC

She always
wears that
same glossy smile,
the curved back,
those red lips,
a statue on a pedestal,
but in time
she too will realize,
especially if she falls,
that she's so hollow
on the inside.

SUNDAY SERMON

I stood there
and the baby
stood there,
both in our
father's pulpit,
me preaching,
he screeching,
and boy
did my
ratings go down
as all changed
their vision
to all in the family
in the front row.

DOWNSTAIRS

Wall to wall carpets,
a spacious living room,
the latest kitchen,
exquisite shower curtains,
but what's in the cellar,
Rita?

FEAR VS. FAITH

"Rabbi, Rabbi
we are lost!"

The windstorm
lashed at the lake,
crashed into our boat.

And Christ said,
"Have no fear.
Have more faith.
Sometimes I come
in the gentle breeze,
but sometimes
I come in the storm."

DINNER FOR SIX

Five of us
sitting here
in the living room,
and you appear
from time to time
in your apron,
with a serving tray
full of hors d'oeuvres and smiles.

And I feel bad
you aren't here
to join our conversation
as you move
back and forth,
from the living room
to the kitchen,
to the dining room,
stirring soup and setting places.

But then,
preparing drinks,
I see your face over the stove,
holding a six way conversation,
nibbling on the words
you stuck your toothpick into
when you came in and served us
all those delicious hors d'oeuvres.

THE LOST SON

Two brothers:
one stayed home,
so the other moved on.
But paths cross,
parents die,
and we all must meet each other
from time to time.

As the younger brother
was standing there
to the right of the casket
his older brother
came in — came in
and refused to shake hands
with either his hands
or his eyes.

Then the younger brother
turned to the casket,
turned to his father,
needing another embrace,
crying at the loss
of what might have been,
remembering the time
their father
tried to get them
to eat the fatted calf together.

NO GRANDCHILDREN EITHER

With two salaries
it seemed much easier
for the young couple
to climb through
the eye of the needle,
especially with
no children
in their arms.
And Jesus said,
"Let the children
come to me."

EVOLUTION

"The photograph is perfect,
except for . . . ."

"Except for what?"

"Well, it lacks . . . ."

"It lacks what?"

"Well, people,
it lacks people."

"There's people, down there."

"Where?"

"Well, you can't see them
from here, but they're there.
God always puts people in the picture."

"Well, when will I see them?"

"Well, as soon as you get closer."

"When?"

"Soon."

LONELINESS

The prospect of loneliness
sits with us
like a silent bird
on a telephone wire
or like the newspaper
tossed on the porch,
obituary column and all.

BEST FRIEND

The man
cut our
conversation off
suddenly, because
his dog just walked in.

Reaching out,
petting the dog,
yelling out,
"Who loves you?"
"Who loves you?"

And all the stiffness
from his face
flowed out
through his hands
into the now
bouncing,
jumping,
dancing dog,
and then he stopped,
and turned back to me.

BROKEN

It broke
as he tried to clasp it
around her neck,
standing there behind her as usual,
making up her eyes in the mirror
before the party —
and without turning she said,
"Stupid!" with her eyes
into the mirror,
and he made up his mind
it was finally broken.

BELOW

Hell,
the underside of ice,
a frozen lake in winter.
Staying here
refusing to look to the sky,
ignorant of the wind,
cutting through
the ice,
to fish, to reach,
still hoping to find
something in the cold
darkness below.

DOROTHY

41 years old:
it was too soon to die,
especially for Dorothy.

She knew how to laugh;
she knew how to enjoy life,
how to take care of her kids,
how to make each day a treat.

Her kids loved her.
She was a "fun teacher,"
as they described her.

And that's how she felt
about life and so she
dragged out her death
for months till she
looked like she was
almost 90.

Cancer can do that.

Months before when she
found out it was terminal
I asked her, "How are you
going to handle this one, Dorothy?"

And with her unique
laugh or cackle
she answered,
"How should I know?"

Well it was 2 weeks
before her death and we
were all alone once again
and this 41 year old nun
answered my original question,
but this time differently,
"Now I know God
has his ways and
I am one of them."

REQUIEM

I just heard the news of your death
from indifferent lips, with words
that held no hint of feeling.

I knew she never knew you,
never shared your presence,
that special way you leaned forward
from the back seat of the car
to tell a story or the way
you always seemed to come up
with quick jokes during
the T.V. commercials.

So I need this time alone to resurrect
the memories you buried within me
during the three years we knew each other.

CLOSER

Another man
moved towards
their table
and at once
he unconsciously
put his arm
around her.
You have
to know
the territory.

LONELY MOMENTS

Lonely moments
in the distance,
only clouds
that pass away?

Or are they
low lying hills
that will be around
for a long, long time?

HESITATION

It was a week
> before my marriage
> and my father
> sat there
> at the dinner table
> and said
> his first "hello."

It was in the form of a question
> and I have forgotten
> the exact words he used,
> but it was his first "hello."
> I was shocked
> and I went to my room crying.

Hesitation set in.
> I exist!
> I exist to the man
> who is my father,
> to the man
> who always just sat there,
> who only yelled at me,
> and that was only
> once in a while.

Hesitations . . . .
Why get married?
Now that my father
talked to me
maybe he's changed.
Maybe he finally realizes
I exist
I am a person.
I have feelings.
I am his daughter.

Hesitations . . . .
While I walked
up the aisle with him,
as he lifted my veil
and kissed me,
as he said,
"Good luck."

There it was for the second time.
He almost said, "Hello."
I almost stopped.
I almost turned around
to walk back down the aisle.
I almost walked home for more.

PAST TENSE

Yesterday,
when I looked back
on my past,
on my life,
I seemed to remember
clearly the twists,
the turns, the mistakes
and the sins.

But today,
thanks to friends,
and so many recent
writers, I'm beginning
to learn
that if I take
a longer look
at my life,
I'll also find some sheep with
the goats, wheat
with the weeds,
and Jesus sitting
there peacefully
within me, the sinner,
and I drop
all these stones,
and all these angry voices
within me walk away
leaving only
scratches in the dust.

UP IN THE AIR

My ears
like hands
keep juggling
your words
as you
toss them
to me,
while your
eyes keep
on juggling
my eyes
to see
if I'm
catching what
you're saying.
Wow! What
a circus!

TAKING OVER

While I was away,
busy, a certain
loneliness arrived
or was it always
there — just outside
the walls of my
life — and now
it came inside
for the winter,
sitting there
in my easy chair,
my favorite chair.

BRIGHT SIDE OR DARK SIDE?

How come the parents
always ask, "Where did we fail?"

Why don't they ask,
"Where did we succeed?"

Could they ask that?
Why do people think it's wrong
to look at their strong points?

Has our religion become only
a fault finder, a garbage
collector, a sin seeker?

Could we have a confession
of our good points?
"How many times did I
help people this week?"

Could we do that?

How fallen is humanity?

ON RETREAT

I sit here wondering
Lord.

Do I want
what you want?

Do I even
want what I want?

Do I know
what I want?

Do I know
what you want?

And I said,
"No."

Do you?

PLEASE TOUCH

Out of touch,
out of touch,
out of touch,
me,
you,
the person
right next to me,
out of touch,
out of touch,
out of touch, but
even when we touch
we seem to be
out of touch.

REASSURANCE

"I know you love me.
That's not what I need.
It's the reassurance,
the reassurance."

EVENING NEWS

He put down the paper;
sitting there in his evening chair,
staring towards the kitchen,
hearing the sounds of her supper dishes,
knowing there was nothing left
but leftovers.

He sat there,
knowing that her headlines
were no longer exciting,
knowing that his day
with her was over.

He worried there,
wondering what the kids now gone
would think, when they
heard the news, knowing
that a divorce
would disturb their evening news.

He stood up,
moving towards the kitchen door
worried how she'd take the news,
but the kitchen was empty.
She had gone, gone
out the back door.

ALWAYS THERE

The death
of a friend
is made of stone.
It is buried
within us
for the rest
of our lives.
The surrounding
weather, the
trees, the
flowers change,
but the stone,
the name,
the date of
the death
remain the same.

HIS AND HERS

From the first date
onwards he always
did the driving.
But slowly
she moved
closer and closer
into the driver's seat,
closer and closer
to him at parties,
till she finally
had the keys,
the wheel and their directions,
and he never knew it happened.
In fact he still thinks
he's doing all the driving,
especially now that
she's moved closer and closer
to the other door,
away from him.

WELL, WE'RE WAITING

Lately,
the word "serve"
has been appearing
all over the place.
A cardinal said that
it was the job of a bishop
and those in authority to serve.
A bishop in Baltimore
might have read that
because he chose as his motto,
"To serve and not to be served."
And I heard a politician
say, "Well, after all,
isn't it our job
to serve the people?"
Then this morning
it was in the gospel,
"No man can serve
two masters."
Well, we're waiting.
Come out, come out
wherever you are.

THE KNOWING

Yes,
death can come
like a surprise postcard
from someone we hadn't
heard from in years.

Yes,
people we trusted
for years can suddenly
divorce us,
cheat on us,
die on us.

But
there is a spring
with flowers
and millions and millions
of birds flying north.

And,
I know Lord
there is You,
and with You
there is a knowing.

TO AN ALCOHOLIC

The speed of the suicide
depends upon the mind of the person.

Just the other day
I was reading in the paper
about this man in Florida
who blew his brains out
with just one shot.
That's all it took,
just one shot.

And as I put down
the paper I wondered
about you sitting there
with another drink
in your hand
and it's not even
noon-time yet.

You'll never make headlines.

But I suppose someday soon
I'll read it in the paper
or hear that you died,
and I suppose very few
will know you've
been blowing your brains
out for years,
yesterday,
today,
everyday,
with many shots.

And I ask myself:
should I tell you what
I'm reading or should
I guess how long it will take?

YOU

The skin of the lake
    shivered and
    became wrinkled
    in the early evening,
    but I didn't notice You
    till a swan
    sailed by.

A CHANGE

Instead of saying
to each other,
"I can't stand you."

Why can't we say,
"I don't understand you."

SLOW DEATH

Sitting there silently
in the back seat,
one arm resting
on his old suitcase,
looking out the window
at his life—a long trip,
memories, friends and funerals,
and work, work, work,
and then slowly
turning into himself,
and then he began
practicing his
nursing home stare
as the car pulled
into the driveway.

OUTLOOK

Cold
and afraid
the snow
rushes across
the fields,
a slave
to the whip
of the wind,
hoping to find
a place to hide
till the spring.

Or,
should it smile
and laugh and
learn to ski
and hope for
a long, long winter?

QUICKLY AND QUIETLY

Please forgive me.
I never really listened
to your words,
to your hopes,
to your jokes,
to your way of seeing things.

No, quickly and quietly
I labeled you that
first time I saw you,
and ever since then
I've kept you in
my "uninteresting" file.

GOING TO THE MICROPHONE

(Ephesians 3:1-7)

The phone calls
to friends announcing,
"It's a girl!"
or "My son is getting
married in June!" or
just stopping in the
supermarket aisle
to exchange the latest news.
But what a privilege
it is to announce
the coming of the Messiah!

QUESTION MARK

Age,
time,
parents' death,
slowing down,
all combined
to cause questions
to kick within me,
a pregnancy,
a birth,
a screaming child
in the night.
And I asked,
"Is this the way
You finally speak
to all of us
who refuse to
speak to You, O Lord?"

A STATUE CALLED ME

What shapes me?
What makes me?

Should I even ask the question?

What are the events, the influences,
the experiences that have shaped my life?

Who have been the sculptors?

What are my dreams,
my fears, my fantasies,
the things that animate me,
the things that hold me back?

What are the assumptions
behind my actions and reactions?

Should I be asking these questions?
Should I make this trip inside myself?

Is the journey worth taking?
Is the journey worth making?

Or is this too much ME,
too much self-absorption,
a narcissism that puts
a mirror before ME
instead of a picture
of all the people in my life?

Did my dad ask these questions
or are they only the trend of this generation?

How do others see me?

Or are they, too, wrapped up in themselves?

EMPTY FIELD

Death,
the pain of loss,
worse than the loss itself,
a parent,
a child,
a loved one,
and the tombstones
kneel there,
row after row,
row after row,
row after row,
dead reminders
that once there was life
in this now empty field.

CLOSED BOOK

There are pages
of me that nobody
has ever read —
pages that I wrote,
pages that are stuck together
and I suppose like
everything else,
it will take
only the knife of pain
to cut them open.

OLD MAN

He was too slow,
not being able
to get into the car
as fast as the others.

Yet as we moved
along his ideas
began to pick up speed
and he made the trip worthwhile.

All he wanted
was a quick trip
to the drug store
for some corn plasters.

But I took
the long way home
just to hear
the end of his story.

LID

A nervous violence
flowed within him,
below his locked mouth,
his tight jaw.
You knew it was there.
You could hear its noise
from time to time,
like a cab going over
a loose manhole cover
in the middle of the night.

AROUND

We walked around
and around the lake.
You said something.
I said something.
But nothing was
connected except
the walk and the lake,
and we'll talk
again tomorrow,
around and around
that same lake.

AVAILABILITY

Availability
is being an umbrella.
You have to do a lot
of hanging around
and then people
curse you when
they can't find you,
and usually they
are the ones who
lost you.

DEJÀ VU

Can't see,
can't hear,
can't speak,
paralyzed,
out of bread,
out of wine,
caught in adultery,
empty net,
looking for a sign,
will he be at the well?

ATHEIST

Sliding, gliding,
across the frozen lake,
past the empty trees,
snow and a below-zero wind,
and I could think of
nothing but the cold,
and in the summer,
different excuses.

THE SLOW AND THE SUDDEN

She died
so suddenly.

What happens
to her plants?

Who will water them?

And what about
her dreams,
her hopes,
her photographs?

She'll stay alive,
a plant watered
by our tears.

She'll remain alive,
a photograph,
constantly being
developed in our dark rooms,
and yet the negative
always remains
the same.

She's dead.

OPENINGS

Windows:
I need those breaks
along the walls
of my life.

Pictures and images
are not enough.

I need more.

I need to see
possibilities,
real ones,
not the ones
on paper,
paintings and photographs
taken by someone else.

I need to be able
to stretch my arms
and my eyes,
to touch,
to grab the stars of night,
to see the pines sweeping the moon,
to fish the seas
and to always find YOU
standing there
on the shore of my life
making breakfast
after a night of catching nothing.

BEGINNING

It's an ugly feeling,
a face-twisting feeling,
this feeling of beginning
again and again and still again.

For the first ten times
it was OK.
I was new.
But now
if I walk out that door
I know I'll be back once again.

I feel like a phony
to myself.

I say to myself,
"OK, here goes.
It's conversion time again.
Up and at them.
Out that door.
Out of this room.
Out to the road.
And get moving
no matter to where
the road takes you."

But I sit here knowing
that soon I'll be back
to this easy chair,
to this easy life.

So why bother opening the door for the 11th time?

I DON'T KNOW

I don't know.

We used to have a fellow
in college who had the
odd nickname of
"I don't know."

He was from Brazil
and whenever he was
stuck in trying to speak English
he'd say, "I don't know."

Well, that's my inner
nickname now, "I don't know."

At first I didn't like it,
but then I read that the
Talmud says somewhere,
"Teach thy tongue to say
'I do not know.'"

Well, I don't know what's
next for me in life.

Is it good or bad to feel
that way?

I don't know.

I DO KNOW

But there are
a few things
that I do know.

I know
that there are a few people
in my life
whom I've met
in my travels,
whom I've learned to know
love me.

And I know
it took me
a long time to realize this:
that I'm loved
and it's a good knowing.

And I know
that I love
a few people
in my life.

Which came first:
the loving or the being loved?

I don't know.

IN CONTROL

The phone rings,
the mail arrives,
the car crashes,
You knock,
and suddenly
I realize
I am not
in control.

OPPOSITES ATTRACT

"18 years of marriage
and you learned nothing
. . . nothing."
She leaned on that word,
"nothing."

And all he could answer
was, "I tried to give you
everything . . . everything."
And leaned on that word,
"everything."

PETER

Yes, I've made many mistakes
in my life. Don't we all?
And yes, my sins were quite
serious. And every time
the cock crows I'm reminded
how I denied him three times
and remember that time I
tried to get him to avoid
the narrow way and take
the wide road home to
safety. And oh yes,
I was bigger on promises
than deliverances — but
wasn't I the one he told
to forgive my brother
seventy times seven times?

DIRECTIONS

Take the turnpike.
Get off at exit 7.
As you come off the ramp
take a right onto Hope Road.
Follow the signs
for Pleasant Valley.
After about three miles
you'll come to a light.
There is a bakery
on your right and
Mary and Louie's Restaurant
on your left.
Turn left at that light.
You are now on Main Street.
Go down about eight streets.
You'll be passing all kinds
of stores on both sides of Main.
You'll come to a
narrow green bridge.
Be careful.
Go over the bridge
and up the hill
till you come to your first
light after the bridge.
Turn right there
onto Paradise Ave.
That's where we live.
We're the third house
on the right.
We'll have a light
in the window
for you.

NURSING HOME

The smell of
urine and silence
filled the place.

They all sat
there near the
elevator, near
the nurse's station,
even though the
chairs were much
more comfortable
in the lounge
down at the end
of the corridor.

They all sat
there waiting
for their kids
to get home from school,
hoping that this time
they would notice
them waiting
at the window,
hoping that their kids
would know
what it means
to grow old and
what it means
to be all alone.

Or is a nursing home
the only school
that gives such a course?

CREATION ACCOUNT

In the beginning
all was God.

In the beginning
all else was silence,
all else was darkness.

And God burst
through the dam
of silence and darkness
with his word,
"Let there be light!"

And God's power,
and God's spirit
exploded into creation.

Molten lava,
red rivers of fire,
huge stones and planets
rolled down the dark hills
of space, down the empty
halls of the universe,
crashing, splashing,
noise and sound.

Creation had begun,
bursting, splattering seed
into the empty holes
of barren time.

"Let there be life!"

And the fertile egg
of earth began.

And in time
the naked baby
came forth
crawling towards
the Father,
standing, falling,
rising, trying
again and again
to stand up
to the Father.

And gradually
it too learned
the words,
"Let there be light!"

ENOUGH'S ENOUGH

The sky kept sending
    snow storm after
    snow storm
    till all was
    filled with white,
    and roads were stuck
    till plowed and salted,
    and then more snow
    was sent in
    gradually covering
    the spirit,
    till the whole village
    cried for spring.

MAGNET

Who
was the first person
to discover
a magnet,
metal attracting metal?
And
who
was the first poet
attracted
to the idea
that people poles apart
could be attracted
to each other?

HAIR

The old woman's hair
    was gray, full
    of cobwebs,
    as if I accidentally
    opened the wrong door
    and found myself
    looking down
    the cellar stairs.

And so I quickly turned
    toward the young
    woman in the
    living room
    with hair like
    surfer's waves
    and blond ski slopes.

And I knew there would be
    no comparison
    at least for
    another forty years.

WATER'S EDGE

I suppose
out there
in the deep
fishes die
of old age
and no one
knows it.
No wonder
they moved
towards shore,
towards man.

ELSEWHERE

Your eyes,
your face
seem so elsewhere.

You seem
so out of place
here with me.

You seem
to be in another room,
in another's eyes.

Where are you?

ABLE TO LAUGH AT ONESELF

We take so many things
for granted. Don't we?

Remember the other day:
me and the toilet paper?

It was missing.
There I sat naming names.

Who did it?

I know who did it.
She's getting so forgetful lately.
And after all I do for her.

But then I suddenly
realized, it was me.

Stupid me.
That's right, it was me.
I put the eight rolls we bought
the other day in the cabinet
in the kitchen
instead of the one here
under the sink.

Well, thank God,
nobody's home.

THE ROOSTER

Christ comes
in the darkest month
of the year: December.

Christ comes
at the time of the long nights.

Christ comes
when coldness
tries every trick it knows
to sneak and creep
through every crack
in our walls trying
to cold warm people.

Christ comes
the best gift of Christmas,
the present from the fireplace,
the Father.

Christ is the rooster
screaming, "It is now
the hour for you
to wake from sleep."

Christ is the rooster
disturbing us with bold
sounds and words,
darting around
the barnyard of earth.

Christ announces
the dawn of a new day.

Christ is the morning
that takes away mourning.

Christ is the rooster
yelling that forgiveness
is always possible
in the morning,
if betrayal took place
in the night.

Christ is the light of day
taking away the darkness
of our December days,
so we can start a new year,
a new life with him,
over and over and over again.

THE LETTER

They were almost home.
It was a long trip,
driving all the way from Florida.

For the last four hours
he was nervous.
The pains in his chest
were getting worse.
He didn't want to scare her
so he said nothing.

They made it,
arriving home
around 3 in the afternoon.

He said he was tired
and needed a good nap
after the trip.

He went to their bedroom,
closed the door
and wrote a long letter —
a love letter to his wife
of almost 30 years.

He wrote how much he loved her,
and how much he appreciated
her caring touch all through
the many years of their marriage.

He said that he had always tried
to help, but if he died
he'd be there
watching over her.

He signed the letter
"With love" and lay down,
still nervous that he might
be about to have a heart attack.

The next day at the doctor's
he found out, "It must
have been gas pains."

It's now 11 years
since all this happened.
The letter is still waiting for her.
It's on top of a similar letter
from his father he found
addressed to him in his father's papers
after he had died about 20 years ago.